This book belongs to:

Dedication

This pottery book is dedicated to all the crafters out there who want to keep track of their projects. Pottery is a wonderful hobby and so fun to do and be creative with. Celebrate your pottery creations with this book.

How To Use This Pottery Project Book

This great pottery project book is perfect for those who love the art and craft of pottery. This book is made for you to record:

Basic Info – Project, Started, Finished, Size, Weight, Clay, Color, Technique, Machine, Firing, Glazing. This is where you can write a great overview of the details of each of your projects.

Sketch/Photo – Either draw your creation or take a photo and attach it.

Additional Notes – A blank space to record thoughts on the process and outcome.

Project Rating – Difficulty, Finishing, Details.

PROJECT		CLAY	
PROJECT NAME		COLOR	
STARTED		TECHNIQUE	
FINISHED		MACHINE	
SIZE		FIRING	
WEIGHT		GLAZING	

SKETCH / PHOTO

ADDITIONAL NOTES

PROJECT RATING

DIFFICULTY	☆☆☆☆☆
FINISHING	☆☆☆☆☆
DETAILS	☆☆☆☆☆

PROJECT	
PROJECT NAME	
STARTED	
FINISHED	
SIZE	
WEIGHT	

CLAY	
COLOR	
TECHNIQUE	
MACHINE	
FIRING	
GLAZING	

SKETCH / PHOTO

ADDITIONAL NOTES

PROJECT RATING

DIFFICULTY	☆☆☆☆☆
FINISHING	☆☆☆☆☆
DETAILS	☆☆☆☆☆

🏺 PROJECT	
🏺 PROJECT NAME	
📅 STARTED	
🚩 FINISHED	
📏 SIZE	
⚖️ WEIGHT	

🧱 CLAY	
🎨 COLOR	
🧿 TECHNIQUE	
⚙️ MACHINE	
🔥 FIRING	
✨ GLAZING	

SKETCH / PHOTO

ADDITIONAL NOTES

PROJECT RATING

💔 DIFFICULTY	☆☆☆☆☆
🏺 FINISHING	☆☆☆☆☆
🗿 DETAILS	☆☆☆☆☆

PROJECT	
PROJECT NAME	
STARTED	
FINISHED	
SIZE	
WEIGHT	

CLAY	
COLOR	
TECHNIQUE	
MACHINE	
FIRING	
GLAZING	

SKETCH / PHOTO

ADDITIONAL NOTES

PROJECT RATING

DIFFICULTY	☆☆☆☆☆
FINISHING	☆☆☆☆☆
DETAILS	☆☆☆☆☆

PROJECT	
PROJECT NAME	
STARTED	
FINISHED	
SIZE	
WEIGHT	

CLAY	
COLOR	
TECHNIQUE	
MACHINE	
FIRING	
GLAZING	

SKETCH / PHOTO

ADDITIONAL NOTES

PROJECT RATING

DIFFICULTY	☆☆☆☆☆
FINISHING	☆☆☆☆☆
DETAILS	☆☆☆☆☆

PROJECT		CLAY
PROJECT NAME		COLOR
STARTED		TECHNIQUE
FINISHED		MACHINE
SIZE		FIRING
WEIGHT		GLAZING

SKETCH / PHOTO

ADDITIONAL NOTES

PROJECT RATING

DIFFICULTY	☆☆☆☆☆
FINISHING	☆☆☆☆☆
DETAILS	☆☆☆☆☆

PROJECT		CLAY	
PROJECT NAME		COLOR	
STARTED		TECHNIQUE	
FINISHED		MACHINE	
SIZE		FIRING	
WEIGHT		GLAZING	

SKETCH / PHOTO

ADDITIONAL NOTES

PROJECT RATING

DIFFICULTY	☆☆☆☆☆
FINISHING	☆☆☆☆☆
DETAILS	☆☆☆☆☆

PROJECT	
PROJECT NAME	
STARTED	
FINISHED	
SIZE	
WEIGHT	

CLAY	
COLOR	
TECHNIQUE	
MACHINE	
FIRING	
GLAZING	

SKETCH / PHOTO

ADDITIONAL NOTES

PROJECT RATING

DIFFICULTY	☆☆☆☆☆
FINISHING	☆☆☆☆☆
DETAILS	☆☆☆☆☆

🏺 PROJECT	
🏺 PROJECT NAME	
📅 STARTED	
🚩 FINISHED	
📏 SIZE	
⚖️ WEIGHT	

🎨 CLAY	
🎨 COLOR	
🧠 TECHNIQUE	
⚙️ MACHINE	
🔥 FIRING	
✨ GLAZING	

SKETCH / PHOTO

ADDITIONAL NOTES

PROJECT RATING

🏺	DIFFICULTY	☆☆☆☆☆
🏺	FINISHING	☆☆☆☆☆
🏺	DETAILS	☆☆☆☆☆

PROJECT	
PROJECT NAME	
STARTED	
FINISHED	
SIZE	
WEIGHT	

CLAY	
COLOR	
TECHNIQUE	
MACHINE	
FIRING	
GLAZING	

SKETCH / PHOTO

ADDITIONAL NOTES

PROJECT RATING

DIFFICULTY	☆☆☆☆☆
FINISHING	☆☆☆☆☆
DETAILS	☆☆☆☆☆

	PROJECT			CLAY
	PROJECT NAME			COLOR
	STARTED			TECHNIQUE
	FINISHED			MACHINE
	SIZE			FIRING
	WEIGHT			GLAZING

SKETCH / PHOTO

ADDITIONAL NOTES

PROJECT RATING

	DIFFICULTY	☆☆☆☆☆
	FINISHING	☆☆☆☆☆
	DETAILS	☆☆☆☆☆

🏺 **PROJECT**		🎨 **CLAY**	
🏺 **PROJECT NAME**		🎨 **COLOR**	
📅 **STARTED**		🧿 **TECHNIQUE**	
🚩 **FINISHED**		⚙️ **MACHINE**	
📏 **SIZE**		🔥 **FIRING**	
⚖️ **WEIGHT**		✨ **GLAZING**	

SKETCH / PHOTO

ADDITIONAL NOTES

PROJECT RATING

🏺	DIFFICULTY	☆☆☆☆☆
🏺	FINISHING	☆☆☆☆☆
🏺	DETAILS	☆☆☆☆☆

	PROJECT
	PROJECT NAME
	STARTED
	FINISHED
	SIZE
	WEIGHT

	CLAY
	COLOR
	TECHNIQUE
	MACHINE
	FIRING
	GLAZING

SKETCH / PHOTO

ADDITIONAL NOTES

PROJECT RATING

	DIFFICULTY	☆☆☆☆☆
	FINISHING	☆☆☆☆☆
	DETAILS	☆☆☆☆☆

🏺 PROJECT	
🏺 PROJECT NAME	
📅 STARTED	
🚩 FINISHED	
📏 SIZE	
⚖️ WEIGHT	

🎨 CLAY	
🎨 COLOR	
🧿 TECHNIQUE	
⚙️ MACHINE	
🔥 FIRING	
✨ GLAZING	

SKETCH / PHOTO

ADDITIONAL NOTES

PROJECT RATING

🧱	DIFFICULTY	☆☆☆☆☆
🏺	FINISHING	☆☆☆☆☆
🏺	DETAILS	☆☆☆☆☆

	PROJECT		CLAY
	PROJECT NAME		COLOR
	STARTED		TECHNIQUE
	FINISHED		MACHINE
	SIZE		FIRING
	WEIGHT		GLAZING

SKETCH / PHOTO

ADDITIONAL NOTES

PROJECT RATING

	DIFFICULTY	☆☆☆☆☆
	FINISHING	☆☆☆☆☆
	DETAILS	☆☆☆☆☆

	PROJECT		CLAY
	PROJECT NAME		COLOR
	STARTED		TECHNIQUE
	FINISHED		MACHINE
	SIZE		FIRING
	WEIGHT		GLAZING

SKETCH / PHOTO

ADDITIONAL NOTES

PROJECT RATING

DIFFICULTY		☆☆☆☆☆
FINISHING		☆☆☆☆☆
DETAILS		☆☆☆☆☆

PROJECT		CLAY	
	PROJECT NAME		COLOR
	STARTED		TECHNIQUE
	FINISHED		MACHINE
	SIZE		FIRING
	WEIGHT		GLAZING

SKETCH / PHOTO

ADDITIONAL NOTES

PROJECT RATING

DIFFICULTY		☆☆☆☆☆
FINISHING		☆☆☆☆☆
DETAILS		☆☆☆☆☆

	PROJECT		CLAY
	PROJECT NAME		COLOR
	STARTED		TECHNIQUE
	FINISHED		MACHINE
	SIZE		FIRING
	WEIGHT		GLAZING

SKETCH / PHOTO

ADDITIONAL NOTES

PROJECT RATING

	DIFFICULTY	☆☆☆☆☆
	FINISHING	☆☆☆☆☆
	DETAILS	☆☆☆☆☆

PROJECT	
PROJECT NAME	
STARTED	
FINISHED	
SIZE	
WEIGHT	

CLAY	
COLOR	
TECHNIQUE	
MACHINE	
FIRING	
GLAZING	

SKETCH / PHOTO

ADDITIONAL NOTES

PROJECT RATING

DIFFICULTY	☆☆☆☆☆
FINISHING	☆☆☆☆☆
DETAILS	☆☆☆☆☆

PROJECT	
PROJECT NAME	
STARTED	
FINISHED	
SIZE	
WEIGHT	

CLAY	
COLOR	
TECHNIQUE	
MACHINE	
FIRING	
GLAZING	

SKETCH / PHOTO

ADDITIONAL NOTES

PROJECT RATING

DIFFICULTY	☆☆☆☆☆
FINISHING	☆☆☆☆☆
DETAILS	☆☆☆☆☆

	PROJECT			CLAY
	PROJECT NAME			COLOR
	STARTED			TECHNIQUE
	FINISHED			MACHINE
	SIZE			FIRING
	WEIGHT			GLAZING

SKETCH / PHOTO

ADDITIONAL NOTES

PROJECT RATING

	DIFFICULTY	☆☆☆☆☆
	FINISHING	☆☆☆☆☆
	DETAILS	☆☆☆☆☆

🏺 PROJECT	
🏺 PROJECT NAME	
📅 STARTED	
🚩 FINISHED	
📏 SIZE	
⚖️ WEIGHT	

🧱 CLAY	
🎨 COLOR	
🏺 TECHNIQUE	
⚙️ MACHINE	
🔥 FIRING	
✨ GLAZING	

SKETCH / PHOTO

ADDITIONAL NOTES

PROJECT RATING

🧱	DIFFICULTY	☆☆☆☆☆
🏺	FINISHING	☆☆☆☆☆
🏺	DETAILS	☆☆☆☆☆

🏺 **PROJECT**	
🏺 **PROJECT NAME**	
📅 **STARTED**	
🚩 **FINISHED**	
📏 **SIZE**	
⚖️ **WEIGHT**	

🎨 **CLAY**	
🎨 **COLOR**	
🧠 **TECHNIQUE**	
⚙️ **MACHINE**	
🔥 **FIRING**	
✨ **GLAZING**	

SKETCH / PHOTO

ADDITIONAL NOTES

PROJECT RATING

🎨 **DIFFICULTY**		☆☆☆☆☆
🏺 **FINISHING**		☆☆☆☆☆
🏺 **DETAILS**		☆☆☆☆☆

PROJECT		**CLAY**	
PROJECT NAME		**COLOR**	
STARTED		**TECHNIQUE**	
FINISHED		**MACHINE**	
SIZE		**FIRING**	
WEIGHT		**GLAZING**	

SKETCH / PHOTO

ADDITIONAL NOTES

PROJECT RATING

DIFFICULTY	☆☆☆☆☆
FINISHING	☆☆☆☆☆
DETAILS	☆☆☆☆☆

🏺 PROJECT	
🏺 PROJECT NAME	
📅 STARTED	
🚩 FINISHED	
📏 SIZE	
⚖️ WEIGHT	

🎨 CLAY	
🎨 COLOR	
🧠 TECHNIQUE	
⚙️ MACHINE	
🔥 FIRING	
✨ GLAZING	

SKETCH / PHOTO

ADDITIONAL NOTES

PROJECT RATING

DIFFICULTY	☆☆☆☆☆
FINISHING	☆☆☆☆☆
DETAILS	☆☆☆☆☆

PROJECT	
PROJECT NAME	
STARTED	
FINISHED	
SIZE	
WEIGHT	

CLAY	
COLOR	
TECHNIQUE	
MACHINE	
FIRING	
GLAZING	

SKETCH / PHOTO

ADDITIONAL NOTES

PROJECT RATING

DIFFICULTY	☆☆☆☆☆
FINISHING	☆☆☆☆☆
DETAILS	☆☆☆☆☆

PROJECT	
PROJECT NAME	
STARTED	
FINISHED	
SIZE	
WEIGHT	

CLAY	
COLOR	
TECHNIQUE	
MACHINE	
FIRING	
GLAZING	

SKETCH / PHOTO

ADDITIONAL NOTES

PROJECT RATING

DIFFICULTY	☆☆☆☆☆
FINISHING	☆☆☆☆☆
DETAILS	☆☆☆☆☆

	PROJECT
	PROJECT NAME
	STARTED
	FINISHED
	SIZE
	WEIGHT

	CLAY
	COLOR
	TECHNIQUE
	MACHINE
	FIRING
	GLAZING

SKETCH / PHOTO

ADDITIONAL NOTES

PROJECT RATING

	DIFFICULTY	☆☆☆☆☆
	FINISHING	☆☆☆☆☆
	DETAILS	☆☆☆☆☆

🏺	PROJECT	🎨 CLAY	
🏺	PROJECT NAME	🎨 COLOR	
📅	STARTED	🤲 TECHNIQUE	
🚩	FINISHED	⚙️ MACHINE	
📏	SIZE	🔥 FIRING	
⚖️	WEIGHT	✨ GLAZING	

SKETCH / PHOTO

ADDITIONAL NOTES

PROJECT RATING

🧤	DIFFICULTY	☆☆☆☆☆
🏺	FINISHING	☆☆☆☆☆
🏺	DETAILS	☆☆☆☆☆

PROJECT	
PROJECT NAME	
STARTED	
FINISHED	
SIZE	
WEIGHT	

CLAY	
COLOR	
TECHNIQUE	
MACHINE	
FIRING	
GLAZING	

SKETCH / PHOTO

ADDITIONAL NOTES

PROJECT RATING

DIFFICULTY	☆☆☆☆☆
FINISHING	☆☆☆☆☆
DETAILS	☆☆☆☆☆

	PROJECT			CLAY
	PROJECT NAME			COLOR
	STARTED			TECHNIQUE
	FINISHED			MACHINE
	SIZE			FIRING
	WEIGHT			GLAZING

SKETCH / PHOTO

ADDITIONAL NOTES

PROJECT RATING

	DIFFICULTY	☆☆☆☆☆
	FINISHING	☆☆☆☆☆
	DETAILS	☆☆☆☆☆

PROJECT	
PROJECT NAME	
STARTED	
FINISHED	
SIZE	
WEIGHT	

CLAY	
COLOR	
TECHNIQUE	
MACHINE	
FIRING	
GLAZING	

SKETCH / PHOTO

ADDITIONAL NOTES

PROJECT RATING

DIFFICULTY	☆☆☆☆☆
FINISHING	☆☆☆☆☆
DETAILS	☆☆☆☆☆

🏺 PROJECT	
🏺 PROJECT NAME	
📅 STARTED	
🚩 FINISHED	
📏 SIZE	
⚖️ WEIGHT	

🟤 CLAY	
🎨 COLOR	
🧠 TECHNIQUE	
⚙️ MACHINE	
🔥 FIRING	
✨ GLAZING	

SKETCH / PHOTO

ADDITIONAL NOTES

PROJECT RATING

🤲 DIFFICULTY		☆☆☆☆☆
🏺 FINISHING		☆☆☆☆☆
🗿 DETAILS		☆☆☆☆☆

🏺 PROJECT	
🏺 PROJECT NAME	
📅 STARTED	
🚩 FINISHED	
📏 SIZE	
⚖️ WEIGHT	

🪨 CLAY	
🎨 COLOR	
👐 TECHNIQUE	
⚙️ MACHINE	
🔥 FIRING	
✨ GLAZING	

SKETCH / PHOTO

ADDITIONAL NOTES

PROJECT RATING

🧤 DIFFICULTY	☆☆☆☆☆
🏺 FINISHING	☆☆☆☆☆
🗿 DETAILS	☆☆☆☆☆

	PROJECT
	PROJECT NAME
	STARTED
	FINISHED
	SIZE
	WEIGHT

	CLAY
	COLOR
	TECHNIQUE
	MACHINE
	FIRING
	GLAZING

SKETCH / PHOTO

ADDITIONAL NOTES

PROJECT RATING

	DIFFICULTY	☆☆☆☆☆
	FINISHING	☆☆☆☆☆
	DETAILS	☆☆☆☆☆

	PROJECT		CLAY
	PROJECT NAME		COLOR
	STARTED		TECHNIQUE
	FINISHED		MACHINE
	SIZE		FIRING
	WEIGHT		GLAZING

SKETCH / PHOTO

ADDITIONAL NOTES

PROJECT RATING

	DIFFICULTY	☆☆☆☆☆
	FINISHING	☆☆☆☆☆
	DETAILS	☆☆☆☆☆

	PROJECT		CLAY
	PROJECT NAME		COLOR
	STARTED		TECHNIQUE
	FINISHED		MACHINE
	SIZE		FIRING
	WEIGHT		GLAZING

SKETCH / PHOTO

ADDITIONAL NOTES

PROJECT RATING

DIFFICULTY	☆☆☆☆☆
FINISHING	☆☆☆☆☆
DETAILS	☆☆☆☆☆

PROJECT		CLAY	
PROJECT NAME		COLOR	
STARTED		TECHNIQUE	
FINISHED		MACHINE	
SIZE		FIRING	
WEIGHT		GLAZING	

SKETCH / PHOTO

ADDITIONAL NOTES

PROJECT RATING

DIFFICULTY	☆☆☆☆☆
FINISHING	☆☆☆☆☆
DETAILS	☆☆☆☆☆

🏺	PROJECT	🎨 CLAY	
🏺	PROJECT NAME	🎨 COLOR	
📅	STARTED	👐 TECHNIQUE	
🚩	FINISHED	⚙️ MACHINE	
📏	SIZE	🔥 FIRING	
⚖️	WEIGHT	✨ GLAZING	

SKETCH / PHOTO

ADDITIONAL NOTES

PROJECT RATING

🏺	DIFFICULTY	☆☆☆☆☆
🏺	FINISHING	☆☆☆☆☆
🗿	DETAILS	☆☆☆☆☆

PROJECT	
PROJECT NAME	
STARTED	
FINISHED	
SIZE	
WEIGHT	

CLAY	
COLOR	
TECHNIQUE	
MACHINE	
FIRING	
GLAZING	

SKETCH / PHOTO

ADDITIONAL NOTES

PROJECT RATING

DIFFICULTY	☆☆☆☆☆
FINISHING	☆☆☆☆☆
DETAILS	☆☆☆☆☆

	PROJECT
	PROJECT NAME
	STARTED
	FINISHED
	SIZE
	WEIGHT

	CLAY
	COLOR
	TECHNIQUE
	MACHINE
	FIRING
	GLAZING

SKETCH / PHOTO

ADDITIONAL NOTES

PROJECT RATING

	DIFFICULTY	☆☆☆☆☆
	FINISHING	☆☆☆☆☆
	DETAILS	☆☆☆☆☆

	PROJECT
	PROJECT NAME
	STARTED
	FINISHED
	SIZE
	WEIGHT

	CLAY
	COLOR
	TECHNIQUE
	MACHINE
	FIRING
	GLAZING

SKETCH / PHOTO

ADDITIONAL NOTES

PROJECT RATING

	DIFFICULTY	☆☆☆☆☆
	FINISHING	☆☆☆☆☆
	DETAILS	☆☆☆☆☆

🏺 PROJECT	
🏺 PROJECT NAME	
📅 STARTED	
🚩 FINISHED	
📏 SIZE	
⚖️ WEIGHT	

🥣 CLAY	
🎨 COLOR	
🧠 TECHNIQUE	
⚙️ MACHINE	
🔥 FIRING	
✨ GLAZING	

SKETCH / PHOTO

ADDITIONAL NOTES

PROJECT RATING

🫙	DIFFICULTY	☆☆☆☆☆
🏺	FINISHING	☆☆☆☆☆
🏺	DETAILS	☆☆☆☆☆

PROJECT	
PROJECT NAME	
STARTED	
FINISHED	
SIZE	
WEIGHT	

CLAY	
COLOR	
TECHNIQUE	
MACHINE	
FIRING	
GLAZING	

SKETCH / PHOTO

ADDITIONAL NOTES

PROJECT RATING

DIFFICULTY		☆☆☆☆☆
FINISHING		☆☆☆☆☆
DETAILS		☆☆☆☆☆

PROJECT			CLAY	
	PROJECT NAME			COLOR
	STARTED			TECHNIQUE
	FINISHED			MACHINE
	SIZE			FIRING
	WEIGHT			GLAZING

SKETCH / PHOTO

ADDITIONAL NOTES

PROJECT RATING

	DIFFICULTY	☆☆☆☆☆
	FINISHING	☆☆☆☆☆
	DETAILS	☆☆☆☆☆

PROJECT	
PROJECT NAME	
STARTED	
FINISHED	
SIZE	
WEIGHT	

CLAY	
COLOR	
TECHNIQUE	
MACHINE	
FIRING	
GLAZING	

SKETCH / PHOTO

ADDITIONAL NOTES

PROJECT RATING

DIFFICULTY	☆☆☆☆☆
FINISHING	☆☆☆☆☆
DETAILS	☆☆☆☆☆

	PROJECT		CLAY
	PROJECT NAME		COLOR
	STARTED		TECHNIQUE
	FINISHED		MACHINE
	SIZE		FIRING
	WEIGHT		GLAZING

SKETCH / PHOTO

ADDITIONAL NOTES

PROJECT RATING

	DIFFICULTY	☆☆☆☆☆
	FINISHING	☆☆☆☆☆
	DETAILS	☆☆☆☆☆

📦	PROJECT	🎨	CLAY
🏺	PROJECT NAME	🎨	COLOR
📅	STARTED	🧿	TECHNIQUE
🚩	FINISHED	⚙️	MACHINE
📏	SIZE	🔥	FIRING
⚖️	WEIGHT	✨	GLAZING

SKETCH / PHOTO

ADDITIONAL NOTES

PROJECT RATING

🧱	DIFFICULTY	☆☆☆☆☆
🏺	FINISHING	☆☆☆☆☆
🗿	DETAILS	☆☆☆☆☆

PROJECT		CLAY	
	PROJECT NAME		COLOR
	STARTED		TECHNIQUE
	FINISHED		MACHINE
	SIZE		FIRING
	WEIGHT		GLAZING

SKETCH / PHOTO

ADDITIONAL NOTES

PROJECT RATING

DIFFICULTY		☆☆☆☆☆
FINISHING		☆☆☆☆☆
DETAILS		☆☆☆☆☆

	PROJECT			CLAY
	PROJECT NAME			COLOR
	STARTED			TECHNIQUE
	FINISHED			MACHINE
	SIZE			FIRING
	WEIGHT			GLAZING

SKETCH / PHOTO

ADDITIONAL NOTES

PROJECT RATING

	DIFFICULTY	☆☆☆☆☆
	FINISHING	☆☆☆☆☆
	DETAILS	☆☆☆☆☆

PROJECT	
PROJECT NAME	
STARTED	
FINISHED	
SIZE	
WEIGHT	

CLAY	
COLOR	
TECHNIQUE	
MACHINE	
FIRING	
GLAZING	

SKETCH / PHOTO

ADDITIONAL NOTES

PROJECT RATING

DIFFICULTY	☆☆☆☆☆
FINISHING	☆☆☆☆☆
DETAILS	☆☆☆☆☆

PROJECT	
PROJECT NAME	
STARTED	
FINISHED	
SIZE	
WEIGHT	

CLAY	
COLOR	
TECHNIQUE	
MACHINE	
FIRING	
GLAZING	

SKETCH / PHOTO

ADDITIONAL NOTES

PROJECT RATING

DIFFICULTY	☆☆☆☆☆
FINISHING	☆☆☆☆☆
DETAILS	☆☆☆☆☆

🏺	PROJECT	🎨	CLAY
🏺	PROJECT NAME	🎨	COLOR
📅	STARTED	🖐️	TECHNIQUE
🚩	FINISHED	⚙️	MACHINE
📏	SIZE	🔥	FIRING
⚖️	WEIGHT	✨	GLAZING

SKETCH / PHOTO

ADDITIONAL NOTES

PROJECT RATING

🧤	DIFFICULTY	☆☆☆☆☆
🏺	FINISHING	☆☆☆☆☆
🗿	DETAILS	☆☆☆☆☆

PROJECT	
PROJECT NAME	
STARTED	
FINISHED	
SIZE	
WEIGHT	

CLAY	
COLOR	
TECHNIQUE	
MACHINE	
FIRING	
GLAZING	

SKETCH / PHOTO

ADDITIONAL NOTES

PROJECT RATING

DIFFICULTY	☆☆☆☆☆
FINISHING	☆☆☆☆☆
DETAILS	☆☆☆☆☆

	PROJECT		CLAY
	PROJECT NAME		COLOR
	STARTED		TECHNIQUE
	FINISHED		MACHINE
	SIZE		FIRING
	WEIGHT		GLAZING

SKETCH / PHOTO

ADDITIONAL NOTES

PROJECT RATING

	DIFFICULTY	☆☆☆☆☆
	FINISHING	☆☆☆☆☆
	DETAILS	☆☆☆☆☆

	PROJECT			CLAY
	PROJECT NAME			COLOR
	STARTED			TECHNIQUE
	FINISHED			MACHINE
	SIZE			FIRING
	WEIGHT			GLAZING

SKETCH / PHOTO

ADDITIONAL NOTES

PROJECT RATING

DIFFICULTY		☆☆☆☆☆
FINISHING		☆☆☆☆☆
DETAILS		☆☆☆☆☆

PROJECT		CLAY	
PROJECT NAME		COLOR	
STARTED		TECHNIQUE	
FINISHED		MACHINE	
SIZE		FIRING	
WEIGHT		GLAZING	

SKETCH / PHOTO

ADDITIONAL NOTES

PROJECT RATING

DIFFICULTY		☆☆☆☆☆
FINISHING		☆☆☆☆☆
DETAILS		☆☆☆☆☆

PROJECT	
PROJECT NAME	
STARTED	
FINISHED	
SIZE	
WEIGHT	

CLAY	
COLOR	
TECHNIQUE	
MACHINE	
FIRING	
GLAZING	

SKETCH / PHOTO

ADDITIONAL NOTES

PROJECT RATING

DIFFICULTY	☆☆☆☆☆
FINISHING	☆☆☆☆☆
DETAILS	☆☆☆☆☆

PROJECT		CLAY	
	PROJECT NAME		COLOR
	STARTED		TECHNIQUE
	FINISHED		MACHINE
	SIZE		FIRING
	WEIGHT		GLAZING

SKETCH / PHOTO

ADDITIONAL NOTES

PROJECT RATING

	DIFFICULTY	☆☆☆☆☆
	FINISHING	☆☆☆☆☆
	DETAILS	☆☆☆☆☆

PROJECT	
PROJECT NAME	
STARTED	
FINISHED	
SIZE	
WEIGHT	

CLAY	
COLOR	
TECHNIQUE	
MACHINE	
FIRING	
GLAZING	

SKETCH / PHOTO

ADDITIONAL NOTES

PROJECT RATING

DIFFICULTY	☆☆☆☆☆
FINISHING	☆☆☆☆☆
DETAILS	☆☆☆☆☆

PROJECT	
PROJECT NAME	
STARTED	
FINISHED	
SIZE	
WEIGHT	

CLAY	
COLOR	
TECHNIQUE	
MACHINE	
FIRING	
GLAZING	

SKETCH / PHOTO

ADDITIONAL NOTES

PROJECT RATING

DIFFICULTY		☆☆☆☆☆
FINISHING		☆☆☆☆☆
DETAILS		☆☆☆☆☆

PROJECT	
PROJECT NAME	
STARTED	
FINISHED	
SIZE	
WEIGHT	

CLAY	
COLOR	
TECHNIQUE	
MACHINE	
FIRING	
GLAZING	

SKETCH / PHOTO

ADDITIONAL NOTES

PROJECT RATING

DIFFICULTY	☆☆☆☆☆
FINISHING	☆☆☆☆☆
DETAILS	☆☆☆☆☆

	PROJECT			CLAY
	PROJECT NAME			COLOR
	STARTED			TECHNIQUE
	FINISHED			MACHINE
	SIZE			FIRING
	WEIGHT			GLAZING

SKETCH / PHOTO

ADDITIONAL NOTES

PROJECT RATING

	DIFFICULTY	☆☆☆☆☆
	FINISHING	☆☆☆☆☆
	DETAILS	☆☆☆☆☆

🏺 PROJECT	
🏺 PROJECT NAME	
📅 STARTED	
🚩 FINISHED	
📏 SIZE	
⚖️ WEIGHT	

🪨 CLAY	
🎨 COLOR	
🧿 TECHNIQUE	
⚙️ MACHINE	
🔥 FIRING	
✨ GLAZING	

SKETCH / PHOTO

ADDITIONAL NOTES

PROJECT RATING

🧤	DIFFICULTY	☆☆☆☆☆
🏺	FINISHING	☆☆☆☆☆
🗿	DETAILS	☆☆☆☆☆

PROJECT	
PROJECT NAME	
STARTED	
FINISHED	
SIZE	
WEIGHT	

CLAY	
COLOR	
TECHNIQUE	
MACHINE	
FIRING	
GLAZING	

SKETCH / PHOTO

ADDITIONAL NOTES

PROJECT RATING

DIFFICULTY	☆☆☆☆☆
FINISHING	☆☆☆☆☆
DETAILS	☆☆☆☆☆

	PROJECT			CLAY
	PROJECT NAME			COLOR
	STARTED			TECHNIQUE
	FINISHED			MACHINE
	SIZE			FIRING
	WEIGHT			GLAZING

SKETCH / PHOTO

ADDITIONAL NOTES

PROJECT RATING

	DIFFICULTY	☆☆☆☆☆
	FINISHING	☆☆☆☆☆
	DETAILS	☆☆☆☆☆

	PROJECT
	PROJECT NAME
	STARTED
	FINISHED
	SIZE
	WEIGHT

	CLAY
	COLOR
	TECHNIQUE
	MACHINE
	FIRING
	GLAZING

SKETCH / PHOTO

ADDITIONAL NOTES

PROJECT RATING

	DIFFICULTY	☆☆☆☆☆
	FINISHING	☆☆☆☆☆
	DETAILS	☆☆☆☆☆

PROJECT	
PROJECT NAME	
STARTED	
FINISHED	
SIZE	
WEIGHT	

CLAY	
COLOR	
TECHNIQUE	
MACHINE	
FIRING	
GLAZING	

SKETCH / PHOTO

ADDITIONAL NOTES

PROJECT RATING

DIFFICULTY	☆☆☆☆☆
FINISHING	☆☆☆☆☆
DETAILS	☆☆☆☆☆

PROJECT	
PROJECT NAME	
STARTED	
FINISHED	
SIZE	
WEIGHT	

CLAY	
COLOR	
TECHNIQUE	
MACHINE	
FIRING	
GLAZING	

SKETCH / PHOTO

ADDITIONAL NOTES

PROJECT RATING

DIFFICULTY	☆☆☆☆☆
FINISHING	☆☆☆☆☆
DETAILS	☆☆☆☆☆

🏺 PROJECT	
🏺 PROJECT NAME	
📅 STARTED	
🚩 FINISHED	
📏 SIZE	
⚖️ WEIGHT	

🪨 CLAY	
🎨 COLOR	
🧠 TECHNIQUE	
⚙️ MACHINE	
🔥 FIRING	
✨ GLAZING	

SKETCH / PHOTO

ADDITIONAL NOTES

PROJECT RATING

🧤	DIFFICULTY	☆☆☆☆☆
🏺	FINISHING	☆☆☆☆☆
🗿	DETAILS	☆☆☆☆☆

PROJECT	
PROJECT NAME	
STARTED	
FINISHED	
SIZE	
WEIGHT	

CLAY	
COLOR	
TECHNIQUE	
MACHINE	
FIRING	
GLAZING	

SKETCH / PHOTO

ADDITIONAL NOTES

PROJECT RATING

DIFFICULTY	☆☆☆☆☆
FINISHING	☆☆☆☆☆
DETAILS	☆☆☆☆☆

PROJECT	
PROJECT NAME	
STARTED	
FINISHED	
SIZE	
WEIGHT	

CLAY	
COLOR	
TECHNIQUE	
MACHINE	
FIRING	
GLAZING	

SKETCH / PHOTO

ADDITIONAL NOTES

PROJECT RATING

DIFFICULTY	☆☆☆☆☆
FINISHING	☆☆☆☆☆
DETAILS	☆☆☆☆☆

🏺 PROJECT	
🏺 PROJECT NAME	
📅 STARTED	
🚩 FINISHED	
📏 SIZE	
⚖️ WEIGHT	

🏺 CLAY	
🎨 COLOR	
🏺 TECHNIQUE	
⚙️ MACHINE	
🔥 FIRING	
✨ GLAZING	

SKETCH / PHOTO

ADDITIONAL NOTES

PROJECT RATING

🏺 DIFFICULTY	☆☆☆☆☆
🏺 FINISHING	☆☆☆☆☆
🏺 DETAILS	☆☆☆☆☆

🏺 PROJECT	
🏺 PROJECT NAME	
📅 STARTED	
🚩 FINISHED	
📏 SIZE	
⚖️ WEIGHT	

🪨 CLAY	
🎨 COLOR	
🙌 TECHNIQUE	
⚙️ MACHINE	
🔥 FIRING	
✨ GLAZING	

SKETCH / PHOTO

ADDITIONAL NOTES

PROJECT RATING

🧩 DIFFICULTY		☆☆☆☆☆
🏺 FINISHING		☆☆☆☆☆
🗿 DETAILS		☆☆☆☆☆

	PROJECT
	PROJECT NAME
	STARTED
	FINISHED
	SIZE
	WEIGHT

	CLAY
	COLOR
	TECHNIQUE
	MACHINE
	FIRING
	GLAZING

SKETCH / PHOTO

ADDITIONAL NOTES

PROJECT RATING

	DIFFICULTY	☆☆☆☆☆
	FINISHING	☆☆☆☆☆
	DETAILS	☆☆☆☆☆

🏺 PROJECT	
🏺 PROJECT NAME	
📅 STARTED	
🚩 FINISHED	
📏 SIZE	
⚖️ WEIGHT	

🪨 CLAY	
🎨 COLOR	
🧿 TECHNIQUE	
⚙️ MACHINE	
🔥 FIRING	
✨ GLAZING	

SKETCH / PHOTO

ADDITIONAL NOTES

PROJECT RATING

DIFFICULTY	☆☆☆☆☆
FINISHING	☆☆☆☆☆
DETAILS	☆☆☆☆☆

🏺 PROJECT	
🏺 PROJECT NAME	
📅 STARTED	
🚩 FINISHED	
📏 SIZE	
⚖️ WEIGHT	

🎨 CLAY	
🎨 COLOR	
🧠 TECHNIQUE	
⚙️ MACHINE	
🔥 FIRING	
✨ GLAZING	

SKETCH / PHOTO

ADDITIONAL NOTES

PROJECT RATING

🎨 DIFFICULTY	☆☆☆☆☆
🏺 FINISHING	☆☆☆☆☆
🗿 DETAILS	☆☆☆☆☆

PROJECT	
PROJECT NAME	
STARTED	
FINISHED	
SIZE	
WEIGHT	

CLAY	
COLOR	
TECHNIQUE	
MACHINE	
FIRING	
GLAZING	

SKETCH / PHOTO

ADDITIONAL NOTES

PROJECT RATING

DIFFICULTY	☆☆☆☆☆
FINISHING	☆☆☆☆☆
DETAILS	☆☆☆☆☆

PROJECT	
PROJECT NAME	
STARTED	
FINISHED	
SIZE	
WEIGHT	

CLAY	
COLOR	
TECHNIQUE	
MACHINE	
FIRING	
GLAZING	

SKETCH / PHOTO

ADDITIONAL NOTES

PROJECT RATING

DIFFICULTY		☆☆☆☆☆
FINISHING		☆☆☆☆☆
DETAILS		☆☆☆☆☆

PROJECT	
PROJECT NAME	
STARTED	
FINISHED	
SIZE	
WEIGHT	

CLAY	
COLOR	
TECHNIQUE	
MACHINE	
FIRING	
GLAZING	

SKETCH / PHOTO

ADDITIONAL NOTES

PROJECT RATING

DIFFICULTY	☆☆☆☆☆
FINISHING	☆☆☆☆☆
DETAILS	☆☆☆☆☆

	PROJECT
	PROJECT NAME
	STARTED
	FINISHED
	SIZE
	WEIGHT

	CLAY
	COLOR
	TECHNIQUE
	MACHINE
	FIRING
	GLAZING

SKETCH / PHOTO

ADDITIONAL NOTES

PROJECT RATING

	DIFFICULTY	☆☆☆☆☆
	FINISHING	☆☆☆☆☆
	DETAILS	☆☆☆☆☆

🏺 PROJECT	
🏺 PROJECT NAME	
📅 STARTED	
🚩 FINISHED	
📏 SIZE	
⚖️ WEIGHT	

🪨 CLAY	
🎨 COLOR	
🧠 TECHNIQUE	
🕹️ MACHINE	
🔥 FIRING	
✨ GLAZING	

SKETCH / PHOTO

ADDITIONAL NOTES

PROJECT RATING

🧁 DIFFICULTY	☆☆☆☆☆
🏺 FINISHING	☆☆☆☆☆
🗿 DETAILS	☆☆☆☆☆

🏺	**PROJECT**	🎨	**CLAY**
🏺	**PROJECT NAME**	🎨	**COLOR**
📅	**STARTED**	🧠	**TECHNIQUE**
🚩	**FINISHED**	⚙️	**MACHINE**
📏	**SIZE**	🔥	**FIRING**
⚖️	**WEIGHT**	✨	**GLAZING**

SKETCH / PHOTO

ADDITIONAL NOTES

PROJECT RATING

🧤	**DIFFICULTY**	☆☆☆☆☆
🏺	**FINISHING**	☆☆☆☆☆
🗿	**DETAILS**	☆☆☆☆☆

🏺 PROJECT	🧿 CLAY
🏺 PROJECT NAME	🎨 COLOR
📅 STARTED	🧑‍🎨 TECHNIQUE
🚩 FINISHED	⚙️ MACHINE
📏 SIZE	🔥 FIRING
⚖️ WEIGHT	✨ GLAZING

SKETCH / PHOTO

ADDITIONAL NOTES

PROJECT RATING

🏺 DIFFICULTY	☆☆☆☆☆
🏺 FINISHING	☆☆☆☆☆
🗿 DETAILS	☆☆☆☆☆

	PROJECT			CLAY
	PROJECT NAME			COLOR
	STARTED			TECHNIQUE
	FINISHED			MACHINE
	SIZE			FIRING
	WEIGHT			GLAZING

SKETCH / PHOTO

ADDITIONAL NOTES

PROJECT RATING

	DIFFICULTY	☆☆☆☆☆
	FINISHING	☆☆☆☆☆
	DETAILS	☆☆☆☆☆

PROJECT	
PROJECT NAME	
STARTED	
FINISHED	
SIZE	
WEIGHT	

CLAY	
COLOR	
TECHNIQUE	
MACHINE	
FIRING	
GLAZING	

SKETCH / PHOTO

ADDITIONAL NOTES

PROJECT RATING

DIFFICULTY	☆☆☆☆☆
FINISHING	☆☆☆☆☆
DETAILS	☆☆☆☆☆

PROJECT	
PROJECT NAME	
STARTED	
FINISHED	
SIZE	
WEIGHT	

CLAY	
COLOR	
TECHNIQUE	
MACHINE	
FIRING	
GLAZING	

SKETCH / PHOTO

ADDITIONAL NOTES

PROJECT RATING

DIFFICULTY	☆☆☆☆☆
FINISHING	☆☆☆☆☆
DETAILS	☆☆☆☆☆

PROJECT	
PROJECT NAME	
STARTED	
FINISHED	
SIZE	
WEIGHT	

CLAY	
COLOR	
TECHNIQUE	
MACHINE	
FIRING	
GLAZING	

SKETCH / PHOTO

ADDITIONAL NOTES

PROJECT RATING

DIFFICULTY	☆☆☆☆☆
FINISHING	☆☆☆☆☆
DETAILS	☆☆☆☆☆

	PROJECT		CLAY
	PROJECT NAME		COLOR
	STARTED		TECHNIQUE
	FINISHED		MACHINE
	SIZE		FIRING
	WEIGHT		GLAZING

SKETCH / PHOTO

ADDITIONAL NOTES

PROJECT RATING

	DIFFICULTY	☆☆☆☆☆
	FINISHING	☆☆☆☆☆
	DETAILS	☆☆☆☆☆

🏺 PROJECT	
🏺 PROJECT NAME	
📅 STARTED	
🚩 FINISHED	
📏 SIZE	
⚖️ WEIGHT	

🎨 CLAY	
🎨 COLOR	
🧠 TECHNIQUE	
🛞 MACHINE	
🔥 FIRING	
✨ GLAZING	

SKETCH / PHOTO

ADDITIONAL NOTES

PROJECT RATING

🧩 DIFFICULTY		☆☆☆☆☆
🏺 FINISHING		☆☆☆☆☆
🏺 DETAILS		☆☆☆☆☆

PROJECT	
PROJECT NAME	
STARTED	
FINISHED	
SIZE	
WEIGHT	

CLAY	
COLOR	
TECHNIQUE	
MACHINE	
FIRING	
GLAZING	

SKETCH / PHOTO

ADDITIONAL NOTES

PROJECT RATING

DIFFICULTY	☆☆☆☆☆
FINISHING	☆☆☆☆☆
DETAILS	☆☆☆☆☆

PROJECT	
PROJECT NAME	
STARTED	
FINISHED	
SIZE	
WEIGHT	

CLAY	
COLOR	
TECHNIQUE	
MACHINE	
FIRING	
GLAZING	

SKETCH / PHOTO

ADDITIONAL NOTES

PROJECT RATING

DIFFICULTY	☆☆☆☆☆
FINISHING	☆☆☆☆☆
DETAILS	☆☆☆☆☆

PROJECT	
PROJECT NAME	
STARTED	
FINISHED	
SIZE	
WEIGHT	

CLAY	
COLOR	
TECHNIQUE	
MACHINE	
FIRING	
GLAZING	

SKETCH / PHOTO

ADDITIONAL NOTES

PROJECT RATING

DIFFICULTY	☆☆☆☆☆
FINISHING	☆☆☆☆☆
DETAILS	☆☆☆☆☆

🏺 PROJECT	🪨 CLAY
🏺 PROJECT NAME	🎨 COLOR
📅 STARTED	🧿 TECHNIQUE
🚩 FINISHED	⚙️ MACHINE
📏 SIZE	🔥 FIRING
⚖️ WEIGHT	✨ GLAZING

SKETCH / PHOTO

ADDITIONAL NOTES

PROJECT RATING

🧱 DIFFICULTY	☆☆☆☆☆
🏺 FINISHING	☆☆☆☆☆
🗿 DETAILS	☆☆☆☆☆

PROJECT	
PROJECT NAME	
STARTED	
FINISHED	
SIZE	
WEIGHT	

CLAY	
COLOR	
TECHNIQUE	
MACHINE	
FIRING	
GLAZING	

SKETCH / PHOTO

ADDITIONAL NOTES

PROJECT RATING

DIFFICULTY	☆☆☆☆☆
FINISHING	☆☆☆☆☆
DETAILS	☆☆☆☆☆

PROJECT		CLAY	
PROJECT NAME		COLOR	
STARTED		TECHNIQUE	
FINISHED		MACHINE	
SIZE		FIRING	
WEIGHT		GLAZING	

SKETCH / PHOTO

ADDITIONAL NOTES

PROJECT RATING

DIFFICULTY	☆☆☆☆☆
FINISHING	☆☆☆☆☆
DETAILS	☆☆☆☆☆

	PROJECT		CLAY
	PROJECT NAME		COLOR
	STARTED		TECHNIQUE
	FINISHED		MACHINE
	SIZE		FIRING
	WEIGHT		GLAZING

SKETCH / PHOTO

ADDITIONAL NOTES

PROJECT RATING

DIFFICULTY	☆☆☆☆☆
FINISHING	☆☆☆☆☆
DETAILS	☆☆☆☆☆

www.ingramcontent.com/pod-product-compliance
Ingram Content Group UK Ltd.
Pitfield, Milton Keynes, MK11 3LW, UK
UKHW022240230426
12048UKWH00018BA/1377